The Water Newton
EARLY CHRISTIAN SILVER

The Water Newton
EARLY CHRISTIAN SILVER

K. S. Painter

Published for
The Trustees of the British Museum
by
British Museum Publications Limited

© 1977, The Trustees of the British Museum
ISBN 0 7141 1364 6
Published by British Museum Publications Ltd.,
6 Bedford Square, London, WC1B 3RA

Designed by M. Leaman

Printed in Great Britain by
J. W. Arrowsmith Ltd., Bristol

Contents

List of illustrations

Preface

In February, 1974, a Roman treasure including thirty gold coins of the fourth century AD was found at Water Newton, near Peterborough. One year later, in February, 1975, Mr A. J. Holmes found by remarkable coincidence in an adjoining field, within the site of the Roman town of *Durobrivae,* a fourth-century early Christian treasure. This publication has been prepared to make the new hoard available for study and discussion as quickly as possible. The objects are illustrated in the condition in which they were found because, at the time of writing, scientific examination and conservation are still in progress.

From the moment of discovery work on the hoard has been a matter of teamwork and co-operation between institutions and individuals. We would like to extend our grateful thanks to all our colleagues in the British Museum and the British Library and also the following: the Cambridgeshire Constabulary; H.M. Coroner for Huntingdon, P. Davies; the Inspectorate of Ancient Monuments, Department of the Environment, especially M. R. Apted and D. Sherlock; the Geophysical Survey Section, Ancient Monuments Laboratory, Department of the Environment, especially A. J. Clark, P. J. Crawshaw and D. Haddon-Reece; the Fitzwilliam Museum, Cambridge, especially Miss J. Bourriau, and R. Nicholls; the Nene Valley Archaeological Research Committee, especially G. Danell, D. Mackreth and J. P. Wild; the Treasury Solicitor's Department; the Victoria and Albert Museum, especially J. Beckwith and C. Blair; and in addition to D. Barag, G. Bonner, D. Brown, J. Brown, R. Bursell, H. Cahn, R. Fellman, Father A. Ferrua, Lord Fletcher, W. H. C. Frend, S. S. Frere, Chancellor E. Garth Moore, R. P. C. Hanson, D. B. Harden, R. M. Harrison, M. Hassall, Father R. Jacquard, E. Kitzinger, P. Lasko, W. H. Manning, M. Martin, A. Oliver, R. Petrucci, R. Reece, A. F. Shore, C. Thomas, F. H. Thompson, E. G. Turner, Miss J. M. C. Toynbee, J. B. Ward-Perkins, W. H. Waterworth and J. Wilkes. The greatest burden of all the work engendered by the find, however, has been shouldered by my colleagues Dr I. H. Longworth, Keeper of the Department of Prehistoric and Romano-British Antiquities, and Miss C. M. Johns, who besides much other work wrote the full catalogue descriptions.

K. S. Painter

Discovery

In February, 1975, a group of one gold and 27 silver objects was found at Water Newton, near Peterborough (Fig. 1). On 10 September, 1975, a coroner's jury declared the group to be Treasure Trove, and it was subsequently acquired by the British Museum.[1] The treasure includes nine vessels and nineteen plaques. Some of the vessels are damaged; but six are more or less complete. One item, a circular disc, is of gold. The other objects are of silver.[2]

The discovery was made by an amateur archaeologist, Mr A. J. Holmes,

Fig. 1 Durobrivae. *Location map.*

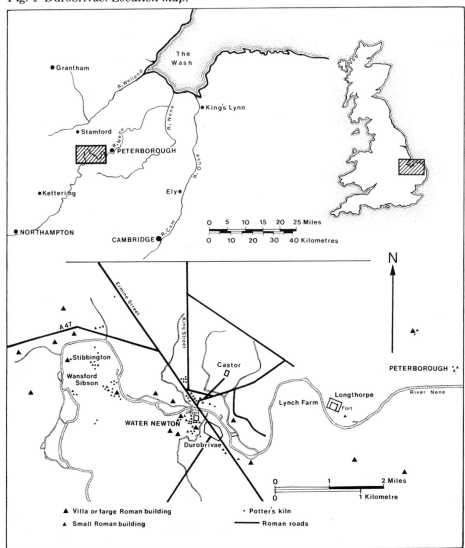

▲ Villa or large Roman building   • Potter's kiln

▴ Small Roman building   ——— Roman roads

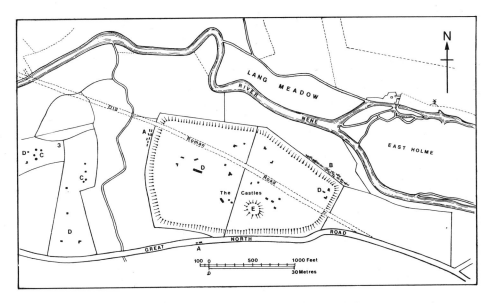

Fig. 2 Durobrivae. *A, B: cemeteries; C: kilns; D: Buildings, (after E. T. Artis).*

just after ploughing by the farmer, in a field which is known to be part of the small Roman town of *Durobrivae* (Plate 30; Fig. 2). Its defences enclose about 17·3 hectares (44 acres). *Durobrivae* lies on the main road between Lincoln and York to the north and London and Colchester to the south. It grew up beside the military fort built in the first century AD to defend the bridge across the River Nene. The importance of *Durobrivae* is belied by it size. Dr Wild has pointed out, 'The residential and commercial buildings so tightly packed within the defences were merely the centre of a much more extensive zone of industrial, commercial and religious enterprise which spread over the old fort site west of the town and across Normangate Field, Castor, north of the river. The suburbs covered at least 100 hectares, an area comparable in size with some of the large towns of Roman Britain . . . The suburbs had begun to grow in the Flavian period and reached their apogee in the fourth century.'[3]

Catalogue

This description of the hoard is arranged so that fact and theory are separated. All entries in the catalogue, as far as is practicable, describe the objects factually and reserve comments and theories for the subsequent paragraphs.

All the objects were examined in the British Museum Research Laboratory in July, 1975, and the preliminary results of that examination are published as an appendix below (pp. 25–6). A full programme of scientific examination and conservation is being undertaken in the Research Laboratory and the Department of Conservation in 1976, and a report of this work will be published in due course.

1 Plain bowl *(Plate 1)*
Damaged silver bowl with slightly everted rim and dished base. Width as found, *c.* 16 cm. (6¼ in.); breadth as found, *c.* 9 cm. (3½ in.); weight (bowl and fragments), 258·3 g. Registration no. P.1975, 10-2, 3. Negative no. (as found): 033436.

The jagged fragment of the rim of this bowl was the first item to be noticed by the finder. Only when he stooped to pick up what he thought was a fragment of pottery did he realise that it was part of a metal bowl. The discovery of the rest of the objects followed; but it was some time before it became apparent that they might be of precious metal and therefore potential treasure trove.

2 Mouth and neck of a spouted jug *(Plate 2)*
Mouth and neck of a large spouted jug, broken from the body. There are several simple horizontal lines encircling the neck; two holes in the rim were perhaps for the attachment of a handle. One small detached fragment survives from the neck.

Height (rim to break), 10·5 cm. (4⅛ in.); diameter across rim, 6·3 cm. (2½ in.); weight (jug and fragment), 151 g. Registration no. P.1975, 10-2, 8. Negative no. (as found): 020775.

Spouted jugs are one of three main types of jug known in the contexts of the fourth and fifth centuries AD.[4] These, however, have bulbous bodies, and the Water Newton jug may prove to have been closer in form to a facetted jug in the Esquiline Treasure which has a long horizontal spout hinged for a lid.[5] In that jug the handle arches above the top of the jug. Ovals on the facets of the shoulder contain letters making up a complete inscription, *Pelegrina utere felix.*

3 Large dish *(Plate 3, Fig. 3)*
A large, deep dish with straight, everted walls and a small, flat, horizontal rim, about 8 mm. wide. The rim is grooved. There is a central depression, 3 mm. in diameter, presumably from turning the vessel, and a second, smaller point close to it, which is in the centre of a broad, circular groove, 11·2 cm. in diameter, and a further grooved circle, 20·3 cm. in diameter. There are areas of concentric, very light turning marks over the whole internal base. In the centre area (the 11·2 cm. circle) is a large, lightly incised Chi-Rho, the rho being of the open form. An omega is present; but there is no trace of the alpha.

Height, 5·3 cm. (2¹⁄₁₆ in.); diameter at rim, 33·5 cm. (13¼ in.); diameter

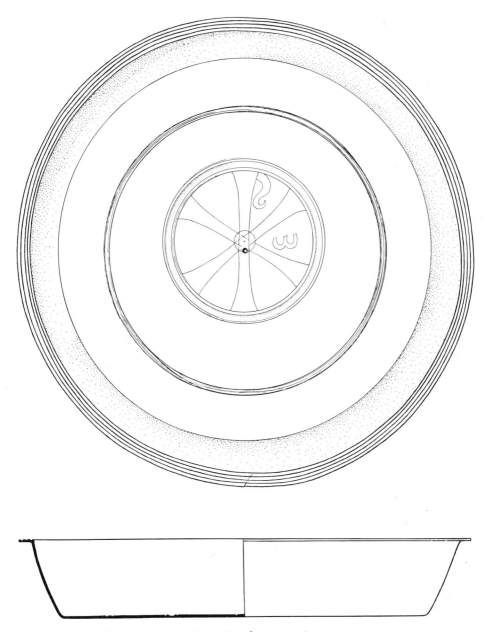

Fig. 3 Large dish. Diameter, 33·5 cm. Catalogue no. 3.

at base, *c.* 27 cm. (*c.* 10¾ in.); weight, 1304·7 g. Registration no. P.1975, 10-2, 7. Negative no. (as found): 020860.

The Chi-Rho symbol is usually assumed to be an indication of a date later than AD 312. The type of rho in this and many of the Water Newton examples is an 'open' rho, in which the curve of the upper part of the letter stops short of the main staff, and sometimes even turns away from it again. The 'open' rho is often claimed to be not earlier than the sixth century; but it is found at least as early as the fourth century.[6]

4 Facetted bowl *(Plate 4)*
Lower area from a bowl in thin sheet silver, elaborately decorated with repoussé worked from the

outside (inside decoration in relief). The vessel is very damaged and there are about fifty fragments from it. The base is slightly dished, and the profile is slightly incurved towards the top, probably with a small, plain, upright or everted rim. Two rings and fragments of chain belong to the bowl. The rings have overlapped ends, like many late Roman finger rings. One, the smaller, is riveted to a portion of the plain rim. The rivet is decorated with a seven-petalled rosette. The zones of decoration of the bowl, from the rim downwards, are: (1) astragalus border between dotted lines; (2) zone of four rows of leaf-tips in scale-pattern; (3) astragali between dotted lines; (4) deep zone of circles with dotted borders, containing five central dots, divided by (a) upright leaf-tips, and (b) opposed peltae with leaf-tips (once only); (5) astragali between dotted lines; (6) as 4, except for pelta motif; (7) three rows of astragali; (8) herringbone pattern; (9) astragali.

Height, *c.* 10 cm. (*c.* 4 in.); diameter, *c.* 18–19 cm. (*c.* 7–7½ in.); weight, bowl and fragments, 220·4 g. Registration no. P.1975, 10-2, 2. Negative nos. (as found): 020782, 020859.

The same kind of ornament punched in from the outside is found on a number of types of bowl of the third century AD. In the Chaourse Treasure, dated about AD 270, there are two bowls so similar in shape and decoration to the Water Newton example that they may even have been made in the same workshop.[7] It is thought that all the thin silver vessels with punched ornament of this type imitate the appearance of contemporary glass-ware.[8] Conclusions to be drawn from the presence of the rings attached to the rim and from the interpretation of the decoration are that the Water Newton bowl was meant to be suspended and that it was the outer

surface, not the inner, that was intended to be looked at.

5 Decorated jug *(Plate 5)*

(a) Silver jug, originally provided with one handle, of which only one fragment (see below) and slight solder marks remain. The marks indicate that the lower attachment was a heart-shaped escutcheon, and marks on the rim show that the handle was horizontal, split and fastened at two points there. The vessel has an everted and upstanding rim, a slender neck, an ovoid body and a high, neatly-profiled foot-ring. The lip is formed simply by angling of the rim opposite the point where the handle was fastened. The neck and body of the jug are covered with zones of relief decoration: the neck has three zones, an upper one of pendant leaf-forms below a roped border giving an ovolo-like effect, a narrow dividing zone of an S-meander between roped lines, and a lower zone of upright leaves of basically acanthus form; there is a narrow plain zone on the shoulder; the body decoration is also in three zones, (1) the upper, on the shoulder, consists of a leaf-scroll with acanthus-leaves and flower-rosettes in alternate curves, the centres of the flowers and the acanthus-buds being decorated with tiny rings, (2) below this zone, at about the point of maximum diameter, is a narrow dividing border like that on the neck—an S-meander between roped lines, (3) the lowest zone, 7·5 cm. deep, contains upright acanthus buds and fully-opened leaves, interspersed with small, simple rosettes.

Maximum diameter, *c.* 11·6 cm. (*c.* 4½ in.); height, 20·3 cm. (7⅞ in.); diameter of rim, 6·5 cm. (2 9/16 in.); weight, 534 g.
(b) Half of a silver handle-attachment from the rim of a vessel. The handle has been wrenched out of the shape when broken. It has a

stylized foliate design, cast and pierced.

Length, 4·8 cm. (*c.* 1⅞ in.); weight, 9·3 g. Registration no. P.1975, 10-2, 1. Negative no. (as found): 020786.

Elements of the decoration can be matched on various types of vessels of several materials and from a wide range of dates. The decoration, therefore, has not yet proved to be of great assistance in pinpointing the date of manufacture of the jug. Dr Barag, however, has pointed out that as a form the jug can be matched in late-third and earlier fourth-century AD glass vessels.

6 Handled cup *(Plate 6)*

Cup of cantharus form with two ogival handles, found detached. There is no decoration, but the external surface appears to have been burnished. The interior shows hammer marks and the position of the handles is indicated by solder marks on the cup. The rim is thickened and neatly finished. The foot is of a low conical form, also has a thickened rim, and is attached to the body by a square-ended rivet. The slight knop between base and cup shows some green corrosion. The handles are of simple, flat section; but the basal attachment is formed to a simple drop-shape.

Height, 12·5 cm. (5 in.); diameter, 11 cm. (4¼ in.); weight, including handles, 315·7 g. Registration no. P. 1975, 10-2, 6. Negative no. (as found): 020784.

The shape of the cup seems familiar; but only one precise parallel is known to me so far, which was pointed out by Dr D. B. Harden.[9] The vessel is a cup found in 1871 at Mzechta, 24 versts north of Tiflis. The cup is of silver with a glass lining and is decorated with a hunting scene. On the basis of the scene Kisa dated the cup to the late-second or early-third century AD.

7 Strainer with handle *(Plate 7)*

A strainer, its bowl pierced with two circles and twelve radiating lines of small holes, each radiating line ending in a group of four holes. There is a separate ring of silver with a segmented pattern on the surface, which fits the rim of the bowl. The handle, which may be partly gilt, has been broken and repaired with three large rivets in antiquity. The handle has engraved decoration, decorative notches along the edges, and at the end a disc, 1·9 cm. (¾ in.) in diameter, bearing an engraved Chi-Rho and alpha and omega within a circle of punched dots.

Length, 20·2 cm. (7⅞ in.); diameter of bowl, 6 cm. (2⅜ in.); weight (including rim), 64·4 g. Registration no. P.1975, 10–2, 9. Negative no. (as found) 020728.

Besides the ancient damage and repair the bowl and handle were glued together after the discovery. A combined strainer and funnel is one of the objects in the Chaourse Treasure, buried *c.* AD 270. A circular casket found on the site of the Walbrook Mithraeum contained a cylindrical strainer with patterned holes on the bottom, which is lifted out by means of crossing bars at the top. A very similar strainer was found at Stráže in Czechoslovakia. The outside of the Walbrook casket is decorated with reliefs showing hunting scenes in a style which seems to relate to the medallions on the hunting dishes from Berthouville and Karnak, and the casket was probably made in the early third century AD.[10]

8 Inscribed cup or bowl *(Plate 8, Figs. 4, 5.)*

A deep, basin-shaped cup or bowl, with a slightly dished base. The rim is everted, with a flat zone beneath, about 2·5 cm. deep, bearing the inscription. The vessel is badly damaged, and only about half remains. One of the broken fragments is from the rim and bears part of the inscription. The lettering

13

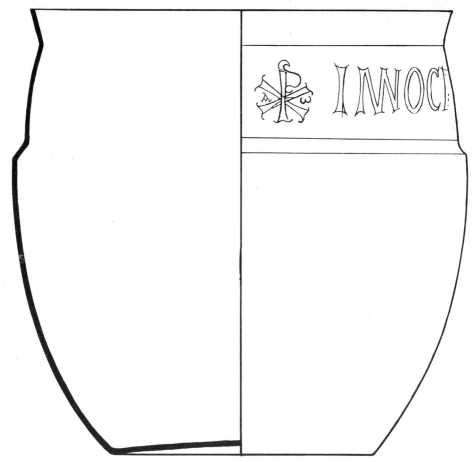

Fig. 4 Inscribed bowl. Diameter, c. 15 cm. Catalogue no. 8.

is double-line in neat letters, about 1·3 cm. high. The Chi-Rho is of elaborate form, with an open rho. The surviving portion of the inscription reads, '(Chi-Rho with alpha and omega) INNOCENTIA ET VIVENTIA . . . RVNT'.

Height, *c.* 12·4 cm. (*c.* 4⅞ in.); diameter, *c.* 15 cm. (*c.* 6 in.); weight including 11 fragments, 260·5 g. Registration no. P.1975, 10-2, 4. Negative no. (as found): 020776.

Three fragmentary letters follow VIVENTIA. They may be the tops of the first three letters of LIB(ENTES). The letters . . . RVNT are part of a

verb, perhaps DEDERVNT, DEDICAVERVNT or OFFERVNT. The choice is uncertain; but the general sense of giving up ownership to Christ is clear.

The inscription is in rustic capitals, probably made from a model supplied by the patron to the client.[11] Rustic capitals are one of the two main varieties of book-hand in use until the fifth century AD.[12] Square capitals are rare, while rustic capitals, made quickly in manuscript with a slanting pen, are the more usual form. Rustic capitals, however, are found cut on

Fig. 5 Inscribed bowl: detail of inscription. Catalogue no. 8.

stone and in other materials, and square capitals equally, designed for use in stone inscriptions, are found to have been used in manuscripts.[13]

The name Innocentia can be paralleled from the neighbourhood of Rome itself. In the cemetery by the Via Appia a sunken area was filled in before the setting up of the Memoria of the cult-centre, perhaps *c.* AD 258. This infill covered three mausolea, of which one was used in the immediately preceding period by a burial-club, the 'Innocentii'. Their club-names, painted in Greek characters on the plaster sealing of their graves, were borrowed from those of the contemporary senatorial emperors of AD 238–244—*duobus Gordianis Innocentiorum, Gordiano Innocentiorum,* and *Popenio Balbeino Innocentiorum.* Cut into the plaster of another chamber of the same tomb was a Christian *graffito* ITXΘΥΣ, combining the familiar Ichthus-monogram of primitive Christianity with a Tau-cross. By the fourth century Innocentii are found in high office in all parts of the Empire.[14]

9 Inscribed cup or bowl *(Plate 9. Figs. 6, 7.)*

A deep cup or bowl, the base dished, with a slightly concave rim. There is damage to one side and to part of the base. A name, facing inwards, is inscribed on the exterior base in neat letters *c.* 7 mm. high—PVBLIANVS. These letters have serifs and are not a rough, scratched graffito. Round the rim is an inscription in letters of the same type and size: '(Chi-Rho with alpha and omega) SANCTVM ALTARE TVVM D (Chi-Rho with alpha and omega) OMINE SVBNIXVS HONORO'. This inscription forms a dactylic hexameter. There are at least three fragments which seem to have the same purplish patination and thickness.

Height, 11·5 cm. (4⅝ in.); diameter, 17 cm. (6¾ in.); weight,

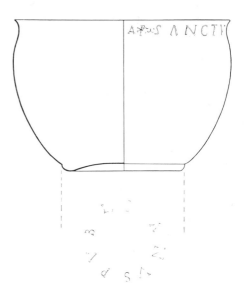

Fig. 6 Inscribed bowl. Diameter, 17 cm. Catalogue no. 9.

including fragments, 662·9 g. Registration no. P.1975, 10-2, 5. Negative no. (as found): 020780.

The sense of the inscription is clear. The name on the base is in the nominative case, not the genitive or dative, and it is not graffito but in the same style as the inscription round the rim. Publianus is therefore most probably the subject of the inscription round the rim, which seems to mean, 'O Lord, I, Publianus, relying on you, honour (or "adorn") your holy sanctuary (or "sacred place")'. Publianus, like Innocentia and Viventia, is clearly giving up his ownership of the bowl. 'Subnixus' has been translated in a figurative sense; but it may equally be used here in a literal sense, 'resting on', 'supported by', or 'leaning upon'.

The hexameter appears to have a false quantity in the last syllable of 'Domine', which falls at the strong caesura. Cameron has shown that there is deliberate, though occasional, lengthening of a short syllable at the strong caesura in the

15

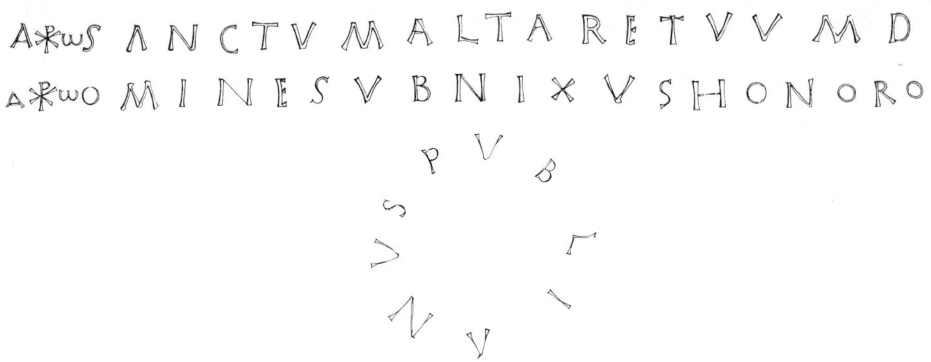

A✶ωS ΛNCTVMALTARETVVM D

A✶ωO MINESVBNIXVSHONORO

P V B
S
Γ
N
V

Fig. 7 Inscribed bowl: detail of inscription on base and round rim. Catalogue no. 9.

approximately contemporary work of Claudian, poet at the court of Honorius (*c.* AD 395–404).[15] Besides the usage of poets like Claudian and Prudentius in traditional forms there must also, of course, be taken into account the use of rhythm in Greek and Latin poetry, certainly in the fourth century and probably from as early as AD 200.[16] In Greek at least this arose at this time from the great problem of the 'new' pronunciation of medieval Greek, which lost the fine distinction between long and short vowels on which the ancient world had based its metric rules. The only possible substitute by which a rhythmic effect could be obtained was the accentuation of certain set syllables in the line and the constant use of the two main ancient caesurae.

The wording of the inscription on the Water Newton bowl is notably reminiscent of phrases in the traditional Mass, such as 'sublime altare tuum' in the 'Supplices', a prayer which is accompanied by the kissing of the altar.[17] The kissing of the altar at various points in the Mass, of which the meaning was later enlarged by the idea that the altar built of stone represented Christ himself, began as a ceremony borrowed from ancient culture. The custom of greeting holy places with a kiss was continued in Christendom, with only a change of object.[18] The same is true of the ceremonies of the introit, in which the elaborations copying

the patterns of the Emperor's court include prostration, to which the word 'subnixus' might conceivably refer.[19] A link between Britain and the eastern rites is not impossible, for Milan has been suggested as the centre of origin of the Gallic liturgy, established by one of Milan's fourth-century bishops who came from the Orient, such as the Cappadocian Auxentius (AD 355–374). This could explain many of the coincidences with oriental usage, more particularly with Antioch-coincidences which are features of the Gallican liturgies and distinguish them from the Roman. Such points of coincidence are the offertory procession after the fore-Mass, the position of the kiss of peace, the *epiklesis.*[20] One of the surviving fragments of a Gallican Mass, moreover, Missa VIII, is in Latin hexameters.[21]

10 Plaque with Chi-Rho (*Plate 10*)
The plaque is an inverted triangle with a central rib and lines in relief, like a leaf or feather. At the upper end is a medallion, demarcated by small repoussé beads, containing a simple Chi-Rho and alpha and omega in relief. In the centre is a small hole, punched from the front. The Chi-Rho, and possibly the background, are gilt. Two fragments are from the tip of the triangle. There is a possibility that No. 11, the gold disc, fits on the back of this plaque.

Height, 13·1 cm. (5¾ in.); width, *c.*

9 cm. (*c.* 3½ in.); diameter of Chi-Rho medallion, 4·8 cm. (1⅞ in.). Registration no. P.1975, 10-2, 10. Negative no. (as found): 020762.

Dated plaques of similar type are rare. Two were found in 1937 at Bewcastle sealed by the fourth-century floor amid third-century rubbish in the underground strong-room in the Headquarters Building of the fort.[22] In Austria, 24 plaques were found at Mauer a.d. Url (Niederösterreich) in a shrine of Jupiter Dolichenus. The cult of Dolichenus was most popular under the Severan dynasty, on the evidence of dated inscriptions of the cult, and so the plaques can be ascribed to the period AD 180–270.[23]

11 Gold disc with Chi-Rho
(Plate 11)
Disc of very thin sheet gold with a central hole 2mm. in diameter. The hole is punched from the side on which the decoration is concave. This is also the side on which the Chi-Rho reads correctly. The open rho has a slight tail. The omega is upside-down. There is a plain circle around the monogram, and a ring of punched dots at the edge.

Diameter, 4·9 cm. (1⅞ in.); weight 4·5 g. Registration no. P. 1975, 10-2, 11. Negative no. (as found): 020732.

The diameters of this disc and the circular medallion on plaque No. 10 seem to correspond, as do also the diameters of the holes punched in them both.

12 Plaque with Chi-Rho and inscription *(Plate 12, Fig. 8)*
Damaged plaque of inverted triangle form. Along the upper edge runs a two-line inscription in relief. The letters are uneven, an initial letter perhaps being missing, and some are mirror-reversed: '... ANICILLA VOTVM QVO(D) PROMISIT CONPLEVIT'. Below this is a hole, nearly 3 mm. in diameter, pierced from the front, and a simple circle in relief, containing a Chi-Rho. The open rho has a distinct tail. The omega is on the left and is upside down in the form M. The left edge of the alpha can be distinguished;

Fig. 8 Plaque with Chi-Rho and inscription. Width, 10 cm. Catalogue no. 12.

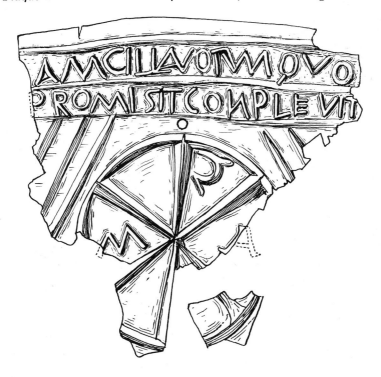

but the letter is mostly broken away.

Width, 10 cm. ($3\frac{7}{8}$ in.); height, 8·7 cm. ($3\frac{1}{2}$ in.); diameter of medallion 5·5 cm. ($2\frac{1}{8}$ in.). Registration no. P.1975, 10-2, 12. Negative no. (as found): 020760.

The name Anicilla was read first as AMCILLA and was thought possibly to be a Celtic name perhaps with the first letter missing at the broken edge of the plaque. Father Ferrua has kindly pointed out, however, that the name can well be read as ANICILLA, a good Latin name with the letters N and I ligatured. For an example of the name see *CIL* II, 3361 (Spain). If Ancilla is a related name, examples are known from Africa: *CIL* VIII 8460—Ancil(1a); 9142—Ancillu; 19103—(An)gilla; 20459—Ancillu; 21634a—Ancillu. A further example of the name 'Ancilla' is to be found on the glass vessel published by de Rossi in 1890: '(Chi-Rho) SANCTO SYLVESTRIO ANCILLA SVA VOTVM SOLVIT'.[24]

13 Plaque with Chi-Rho *(Plate 13)*
Plaque of inverted triangle form with 'leaf' or 'feather' pattern radiating to each corner. There is a pinhole in the centre of the Chi-Rho and in the lower point. The Chi-Rho is surrounded by a circle in relief. The rho is mirror-reversed, and the omega, which is on the left, is shaped like an E on its side.

Height, 11·2 cm. ($4\frac{3}{8}$ in.); 10·5 cm. ($4\frac{1}{8}$ in.); diameter of medallion, 5·5 cm. ($2\frac{1}{4}$ in.). Registration no. P.1975, 10–2, 13. Negative no. (as found): 020757.

14 Plaque with Chi-Rho *(Plate 14)*
Small triangular plaque with leaf patterns in the corners only. No pinhole. There is a simple repoussé Chi-Rho within a plain circle. The open rho has a tail. The outlines of the alpha have been sharpened by scratches on the right side. There is a slightly yellowish patina over the whole surface, which may be

tarnish or the remains of thin gilding.

Height, 6·7 cm. ($2\frac{5}{8}$ in.); width, 5.9 cm. ($2\frac{5}{16}$ in.); diameter of medallion, 3·8 cm. ($1\frac{1}{2}$ in.). Registration no. P.1975, 10-2, 14. Negative no. (as found): 020734.

15 Plaque *(Plate 15)*
Narrow triangular plaque, presumably broken, with central rib and lines in a leaf or feather-pattern. A hole, *c.* 3 mm. in diameter, has been pierced from the back.

Height, 7·4 cm. ($2\frac{15}{16}$ in.); width, *c.* 4·5 cm. (*c.* $1\frac{3}{4}$ in.). Registration no. P.1975, 10-2, 15. Negative no. (as found): 020735.

16 Plaque with Chi-Rho *(Plate 16)*
Small triangular plaque, with relief 'leaf' patterns in the corners. A small circle contains a simple Chi-Rho without alpha and omega. The open rho has a slight tail. A small hole in the centre of the Chi-Rho is pierced from the back.

Height, 6·8 cm. ($2\frac{3}{4}$ in.); width, 5·2 cm. ($2\frac{1}{16}$ in.); diameter of medallion 2·5 cm. (1 in.). Registration no. P.1975,10-2, 16. Negative no. (as found): 020747.

17 Plaque *(Plate 17)*
Small, broken triangular plaque with leaf pattern in relief, and a hole in the central rib, pierced from the back.

Height, 7·8 cm. ($2\frac{5}{8}$ in.); width, *c.* 4 cm. (*c.* $1\frac{5}{8}$ in.). Registration no. P. 1975, 10-2, 17. Negative no. (as found): 020746.

18 Plaque with Chi-Rho *(Plate 18)*
Triangular plaque with repoussé leaf or feather pattern. A large gilt medallion contains a Chi-Rho in very bold relief, with alpha and omega. The open rho has a tail.

Height, 15·7 cm. ($6\frac{1}{8}$ in.); width, 11·3 cm. ($4\frac{1}{2}$ in.); diameter of medallion, 7 cm. ($2\frac{3}{4}$ in.). Registration no. P.1975, 10-2, 18. Negative no. (as found): 020756.

19 Plaque with Chi-Rho *(Plate 19)*
Small triangular plaque with leaf pattern. The Chi-Rho is a simple one, the rho being without the added tail, and the alpha having a dot rather than a cross-bar. There is no hole pierced in the plaque.

Height, 4·9 cm. ($1\frac{15}{16}$ in.); width, 3·5 cm. ($1\frac{3}{8}$ in.); diameter of medallion, 2·5 cm. (1 in.). Registration no. P.1975, 10–2, 19. Negative no. (as found): 020743.

20 Plaque *(Plate 20)*
Damaged triangular plaque, with repoussé ribs in leaf or feather-pattern. There is no hole pierced in the plaque.

Height, 5·8 cm. ($2\frac{1}{4}$ ins.); width, 3·8 cm. ($1\frac{1}{2}$ in.). Registration no. P. 1975, 10-2, 20. Negative no. (as found): 020740.

21 Plaque with Chi-Rho *(Plate 21)*
Triangular plaque with the point upwards, decorated with a leaf-pattern. A medallion contains a Chi-Rho; this is in intaglio and the alpha and omega are in relief. Following the sides of the plaque next to the medallion is a border of small beads. The rho has a tail.

Height, 6 cm. ($2\frac{3}{8}$ in.); width, *c.* 4·5 cm. (*c.* $1\frac{3}{4}$ in.); diameter of medallion, 2·8 cm. ($1\frac{1}{8}$ in.). Registration no. P. 1975, 10-2, 21. Negative no (as found): 020741.

22 Plaque with Chi-Rho *(Plate 22)*
Triangular plaque, point upwards. The upper part has repoussé ribs in a leaf pattern. The Chi-Rho medallion is in relief, but has no bold outer circle, merely a line incised on the back. The open rho has a tail, the alpha is of a somewhat distorted form. In the lower two corners of the plaque are two small fronds or leaves, and there are beaded borders following the plaque edges in the lower area.

Height, 8 cm. ($3\frac{1}{8}$ in.); width, 6·4 cm. ($2\frac{1}{2}$ in.); diameter of the medallion, 4·2 cm. ($1\frac{5}{8}$ in.).

Registration no. P.1975, 10-2, 22. Negative no. (as found) 020738.

23 Plaque *(Plate 23)*
Triangular plaque with ribbed pattern based on lines into each corner.

Height, 7 cm. ($2\frac{3}{4}$ in); width, 6 cm. ($2\frac{3}{8}$ in.). Registration no. P.1975, 10-2, 23. Negative no. (as found): 020751.

24 Plaque *(Plate 24)*
Fragment of triangular 'leaf' or 'feather' plaque with ribs.

Height, 3·8 cm. ($1\frac{1}{2}$ in.); width, 2·9 cm. ($1\frac{1}{8}$ in.). Registration no. P.1975, 10-2, 24. Negative no. (as found): 020749.

25 Plaque *(Plate 25)*
Triangular plaque with rather faint leaf pattern.

Height, 8 cm. ($3\frac{1}{8}$ in.); width, 4·5 cm. ($1\frac{3}{4}$ in.). Registration no. P. 1975, 10-2, 25. Negative no. (as found): 020754.

26 Plaque *(Plate 26)*
Small triangular plaque with bold centre rib and lines. There is a small hole pierced near the base of the triangle.

Height, 5·6 cm. ($2\frac{1}{4}$ in.); width, 2·4 cm. ($\frac{15}{16}$ in.). Registration no. P.1975, 10-2, 26. Negative no. (as found): 020766.

27 Plaque *(Plate 27)*
Damaged triangular plaque with ribs in leaf or feather pattern.

Height, 7 cm. ($2\frac{3}{4}$ in.); width, 4 cm. ($1\frac{5}{8}$ in.). Registration no. P.1975, 10-2, 27. Negative no. (as found), 020764.

28 Fragments
Thin silver sheet, 13 pieces of which show some joins, plus about thirty miscellaneous pieces, some minute. None of these is decorated in any way.

There are also numerous broken fragments from triangular leaf plaques.

Date and cause of the deposit

There is evidence that the vessels were not abandoned but were put away with the intention of being recovered. First, the finder described how the vessels lay carefully arranged in the large dish (Plate 28), and his evidence is confirmed by marks on the dish (Plate 4). The bright patches, for example, show that some of the plaques lay directly on the dish (Plate 29). Second, scientific examination of the broken edges of the objects shows that the majority of the breaks are recent and likely to have occurred during ploughing or the removal of the objects from the soil. All the objects, therefore, were probably in a usable condition when they were put away in antiquity, even though the fact that the handles had been deliberately taken off the two-handled cup shows that immediate re-use was not contemplated (Plate 6).

The problems of the reasons for the deposition and its date are closely linked. One possible reason for hiding religious objects might be to protect them from damage by members of other cults. This is supported by evidence in Britain for the destruction of several of the five excavated temples of Mithras, probably by Christians. At the temple in London the threat of serious trouble caused the Mithraists to bury some of their chief treasures in two groups in the north-west corner of the nave about the middle of the fourth century. That the source of trouble was zealous Christians is suggested by fragments of broken statuary at this level and by the removal of the columns, perhaps for re-use in a church. At Caernarvon the Tauroctony, the dadophori and the inscribed altars were removed, and this shows that the temple was probably abandoned when the garrison was withdrawn about AD 290; but, when the garrison returned about AD 350, the remaining small altars were smashed and the building burnt down, very probably by Christian soldiers. At both Carrawburgh and Rudchester the Tauroctony was removed or almost entirely destroyed, the figures of the dadophori were deliberately smashed, but the altars were left alone. Since this is not the action of Mithraists closing down their temple, nor the work of invaders, who would not be selective, it was probably the result of Christian activity. The similarity of treatment at both temples, and the coin evidence, suggest that both were attacked in the same wave of feeling, about AD 310–320.[25]

The Christians were similarly subject to attack, both unofficial and official. In the third century, for example, persecutions of the Christians were initiated by Maximinus Thrax in AD 235, by Decius in AD 250, and by Valerian in AD 257 and 258. Gallienus, however, in AD 260 cancelled the measures of his predecessor, restored church property, and ushered in a long period of peace. Diocletian (AD 284–305) at first continued the policy of his predecessors Gallienus and Aurelian; but in AD 303 and 304 he launched the Great Persecution, and attacks on the church continued until the edicts of toleration of Galerius in AD 311 and of Maximin in AD 313 agreed to recognise the legal personality of the Christian Churches and to tolerate all religions equally.[26] Christians in Britain suffered in such attacks, both official and unofficial, for which the martyrdoms of St Alban and of Aaron and Julius are primary evidence.[27] Christian objects and buildings in Gaul and Britain were equally subject to the regulations of persecutions like that of Diocletian, and evidence from North Africa shows that it was important to remove writings and objects from Christian buildings, to protect both the buildings from destruction and all the objects within the building, whether Christian or not, from confiscation by the authorities.[28] Constantius Chlorus, Augustus of the western half of the Empire at the time of the Great Persecution, may well have avoided any bloodshed in his territory; but the evidence seems clear that he did destroy property, and this sort of action or even the fear of it, would have been good reason to hide the Water Newton Treasure, no matter whether the concealment was at this precise time in the fourth century or not.[29]

Protection from persecution by other cults is not the only possible reason for the concealment of precious objects. Protection from theft or protection against raids from outside the Empire could have been equally strong motives to hide the Water Newton silver in some way. A Berlin papyrus of the first century BC, or first century AD, preserves the inventory of plate which a wealthy Roman in Egypt had packed in chests and deposited in various hands for safe-keeping.[30] This is just the same method of safe-keeping as that employed by Mensurius, Bishop of Carthage, in AD 308.[31] Many more examples of such concealment can be quoted in the cases of coin hoards. A large number of the hoards that have come to light, however, were buried in some time of crisis to prevent them from falling into the hands of an enemy from outside the Empire. A hoard of first-century silver from Hockwold in Norfolk discovered in 1962 has been connected with Boudicca's rebellion.[32] Most of the major finds have some similar historical explanation. The two main groups of hoards are those connected with barbarian invasions in the late third century and those buried in the later fourth and early fifth centuries. One of the largest and most important hoards of the third century is the Treasure of Berthouville from the site of a Temple of Mercury destroyed at that time.[33] Another large hoard is the Treasure of Chaourse, a large find of domestic plate which had been buried wrapped in cloth.[34] The latest coins found with the silver belonged to the reign of Postumus (AD 267), and the treasure was probably buried about AD 270. Fourth- and fifth-century hoards include those from Kaiseraugst, Switzerland, from Mildenhall, Suffolk, and the Esquiline Hill in Rome.[35] One of the most striking recent discoveries of this type is from Water Newton itself, a treasure which was found in 1974 in a field outside the walls of *Durobrivae*, and which includes both silver plate and also gold coins which date the deposit to AD 350 (Plates 31–35; Figs. 9–11).[36] This was the beginning of a period of fifteen years when the Roman army in Britain was unable to control its foes.[37]

For which of these three major possible reasons and at what precise date the Water Newton Christian Treasure was buried it is not at present possible to say; but the hoard does include types of vessel made in the third century, the vessels were not broken up like those of the fifth-century hoards from Traprain Law in Scotland, Coleraine in Ireland, Gross Bodungen in Germany and Høstentorp in Denmark, and the vessels were complete when buried, like those in the hoards of Mildenhall, Kaiseraugst, Carthage and the Esquiline Hill. The Water Newton hoard, however, does not include types to be found in these latter hoards from the later part of the fourth century. The Water Newton Christian Treasure, therefore, was deposited probably in the fourth century, and perhaps in the earlier rather than the later part of that century.[38]

Character and use of the Treasure

In character the treasure is religious and not secular. There is no apparent reason why the vessels should not occur as types in any of the secular hoards of the period. Indeed, the facetted bowl (Plate 4) may have come from the same workshop as those in the treasure of Chaourse. Unlike modern church plate, vessels in antiquity were not of distinctive form and sacred by consecration. They acquired their character from the authority of the person using them. This difference is illustrated by an incident in the quarrel between St Athanasius and the Meletians.[39] In AD 332 Athanasius was summoned to the court at Nicomedia, and the charges against him were tried before the Emperor himself in the Palace of Psammathia. He was accused of having sent a purse of gold as a bribe to one Philumenus, probably Master of the Offices, and of sacrilege. The prosecution alleged that when Athanasius was making one of his regular visitations of the Mareotes, he dispatched one of his priests named Macarius to summon before him a priest named Ischyras: Macarius burst in while Ischyras was celebrating, overturned his altar, smashed his chalice and burnt his books. Athanasius' story was that the prosecution's account was not true; but that, even if it had been, Ischyras was not a genuine priest because he had been ordained by a priest who had not been properly appointed bishop; that therefore there was not and never had been any church in Ischyras' village—his church was a small dwelling-house; and as for the chalice, 'there are many cups in private houses and in the market, and there is no sacrilege in breaking any of these; but the mystic cup, which if it is deliberately broken, involves the perpetrator in sacrilege, is found only in the possession of lawful priests'. Athanasius was triumphantly acquitted. The religious nature, therefore, of the vessels in the Water Newton Treasure is to be adduced only from their association within the whole group and from the internal evidence, such as the inscriptions, not through any difference of form which can distinguish them visibly from vessels made and sold for other, secular, purposes. The plaques in the Water Newton Treasure, however, can only be religious (Plates 10–27). Such plaques are known from the western to the eastern ends of the Roman Empire.[40] All previous discoveries, however, are pagan. The Water Newton plaques are of exactly the same type, but they are the first to be discovered with Christian symbols and inscriptions; they are votive, and the inscriptions on two of the vessels show that in their case, too, the persons named had given up ownership of them. The three major inscriptions and the use, fifteen times, of the Chi-Rho device demonstrate that the whole Water Newton Treasure is religious and Christian.

The use of the Water Newton Treasure is problematical. The plaques are clearly votive—payments to God for requests fulfilled—but the group of vessels overall must be compared with those in other major hoards of the period. They resemble the pieces in the important religious hoard from Berthouville in France in that they have dedicatory inscriptions, but the latter were old and more or less worn when the dedications to Mercury were added in the third century AD. The major secular hoards known were all usable when deposited, yet the Water Newton Treasure, by contrast, was both religious and in good usable condition when buried. Unlike the secular pieces, however, no vessel has inscriptions of possession or weight scratched on it. The treasure seems likely, therefore, to have been in the possession of, and being used by, a practising Christian group, perhaps for *refrigeria* or for baptism or for Communion.[41] Before the third century the material gifts of bread and wine by the laity were hardly ever mentioned, only the thanksgiving over them; but from the third century it is precisely the material side which is stressed. Bread and wine are referred to, for example by Cyprian, as the *sacrificium*.[42] It was not long, however, before the offerings consisted of objects other than bread and wine.[43] From the era of Constantine we have the mosaic from the floor of the large double church excavated at Aquileia; here is the representation of an offertory procession in which men and women are bringing not only bread and wine, but also grapes, flowers and a bird. For that reason it became necessary from early times to make regulations specifying in what manner these offerings could be made. A Synod of Hippo in AD 393 says categorically: 'At the Sacrament of the Body and Blood of Christ nothing is to be offered except bread and wine mixed with water.' About the same time the Apostolic Canons stipulate: 'When a bishop or priest, offers up something else: honey or milk, or, in place of (the right kind), wine turned to vinegar, or fowl, or any type of feast or vegetable, in opposition to the mandate, he should be deposed. Aside from the ears of wheat and grapes in season and oil for the lamps and incense, nothing should be brought to the altar at the time of the sacrifice. All other fruits should (as firstlings) be sent to the bishop or the priests at their home and not to the altar; it is clear that the bishop and priests distribute these too among the deacons and other clergy.' These ordinances were repeated and expanded also in the West during the ensuing centuries. Amongst the objects meriting the honour of being allowed to be brought to the altar, there appear, in addition to the oil for the lamps, especially wax and candles. Next we hear that in many churches 'precious ecclesiastical furnishings' destined for the church were laid on the altar at the offertory procession on great feasts. Even the transfer of immovable property was often executed by handing over a deed or voucher at the offertory.

There seems little reason to doubt, therefore, that new recruits to Christianity felt encouraged to bring offerings of pagan type, their *oblationes*, to place within the *altare,* not the altar, but the sanctuary or sacred place.[44] Annexes in pagan temples, which may have been used for precisely the reception and display of offerings, are known both in Britain and in other parts of the Empire.[45] Other areas of activity in which paganism and Christianity came together, particularly after the Edict of Milan, are architecture, music, and the language and style of prayers, while the court of the Roman Emperor was another source from which various customs of ancient Roman culture—including emperor-worship—flowed into the Christian liturgy.[46] We must not lose sight, however, of the real possibility that the long inscription of Publianus on the deep cup or bowl (Plate 9) both attests the existence of some structure implied by the word *'altare',* and also might even be a direct quotation from some form of the mass.[47]

Conclusion

It is not known whether the Water Newton Christian silver was in a shrine or church at *Durobrivae. Durobrivae,* however, does lie on the main road between Lincoln and York to the north and London and Colchester to the south, and so the objects could have been hidden while in passage between these places. Further, Publianus, Innocentia, Viventia and Anicilla may not even have had a particularly close personal connection with Britain at all, for the estates of great private landlords were often scattered over many provinces.[48] A particular example is Melania the younger, a lady of a great Roman family, and her equally noble husband, Pinianus, who in AD 404, decided to sell all their goods and give the money to the poor, and who later settled in Palestine. Her biographer draws a vivid picture of her making a leisurely progress from Rome to Carthage, systematically selling her estates in Campania, Apulia, Sicily, Africa, Numidia, and Mauretania: she also owned lands in Spain and in Britain itself.[49] The size of some of her individual estates was vast. She endowed the church of Tagaste in Africa with an estate which was larger than the city itself, 'with a villa and many craftsmen, gold, silver and coppersmiths, and two bishops one of our faith and one of the heretics'. From the names in the Water Newton Christian Treasure, however, and from the use of Latin, what does seem clear is that the hoard belongs in the western half of the Roman Empire, even though the type of Chi-Rho device and the double-stroke lettering suggest an eastern origin for the workmanship.[50]

Before the discovery of the Water Newton Christian Treasure the two earliest known Christian religious treasures were those of Canoscio in Umbria, and of Kumluca in south-west Turkey, both of the sixth century AD.[51] The Water Newton silver is not later than the fourth century AD. The group includes religious plaques which are pagan in type and vessels which are ordinary secular types used for Christian religious purposes. The objects throw light on areas of the history of Christianity of which we know almost nothing. The Water Newton treasure is the earliest known group of Christian silver from the whole Roman Empire.

APPENDIX A: Preliminary Scientific Examination and Report of the British Museum Research Laboratory

by H. Barker, M. R. Cowell, P. T. Craddock, M. J. Hughes and Janet Lang.

The work included visual examination under a high-power microscope, spectrographic analysis of all the items in the hoard, quantitative analysis by atomic absorption on two of the major pieces, and microscopic examination of the soils adhering to some of the hoard.

A Material
All the objects are of silver with the exception of the gold disc (Catalogue no. 11; Registration no. P.1975, 10-2, 11). The rivet inside the cup (Catalogue no. 6; Registration no. P.1975, 10-2, 6), which is covered in green corrosion products, appears to be a silver-copper alloy (i.e. debased silver). The silver of bowls nos. 8 (Registration no. P.1975, 10-2, 4) and 9 (Registration no. P.1975, 10-2, 5) have been analysed quantitatively and showed the presence in bowl no. 8 of 2·4% copper and 0·5% tin (i.e. silver, 97%) and in bowl no. 9 of 4·0% copper and 0·1% tin (i.e. silver, 96%). The silver is therefore of a high standard. Without further quantitative analysis it is not possible to tell whether any other objects in the hoard are of the same high standard of silver. The total weight of the silver is 3977 g., and of the gold plaque 4·5 g.

B Physical Examination
Of the major vessels three are very badly damaged (bowls nos. 1 and 8 and dish no. 3—Registration nos. P.1975, 10-2, 3, 4 and 2). It is obvious that a considerable amount of these vessels is still missing, even if all the other fragments found with the hoard are taken into account. Some objects have heavy score marks on their surfaces which have been made by turning on a lathe. Microscopic examination of the bowls and fragments shows that the nature of the score marks from the lathe is characteristic of each bowl, and thus the fragments can in some cases be matched to the respective bowl on the basis of these score marks. Examination of the broken edges under the microscope, both of the bowls and of the associated fragments, shows that the majority of the breaks are recent, i.e. made during ploughing or removal of the objects from the soil. There appear to be more of these recent breaks than can be accounted for by reconstructing the bowls as they stand at the moment. The conclusion drawn is that the bowls were damaged recently, and while some of the fragments have been recovered, there are still other fragments not accounted for.

   Physical and metallographic examination has been carried out on eight of the major pieces in the Water Newton hoard, as well as on a selection of the plaques. Objects 1, 5, and 7 need to be examined again after cleaning. It was not possible to examine object 9 at this stage.

1 Plain bowl
The bowl had been raised and then scraped on a lathe. The outer surface was then polished; the rim was hammered down to neaten and thicken it.

2 Mouth and neck of spouted jug
The jug was made by raising: anvil marks can be seen on the inside surface. The outer surface has been finished on a lathe and polished. Decorative lines were inscribed on the surface, possibly on the lathe. This operation took place before the final anneal. Holes near the top were made by a round-ended punch from the outside. The top edge of the jug seems to have been filed and the pouring lip worked outwards on an anvil. The metal is in a brittle state with intercrystalline corrosion.

3 Large dish
This was made by raising, and finished on the inner surface by scraping and polishing. Decoration was by scribed lines, two centres being used. There are faint traces of letters which could be examined after cleaning.

4 Facetted bowl

This bowl was made by raising with frequent anneals. The surface was then scraped, using a lathe to rotate the bowl, after which the decoration was introduced, using a series of different sized punches. A chain made from wire which had not been drawn (in the modern sense) but possibly hammered or swaged from a strip of sheet, was attached by means of a decorated rivet.

5 Decorated jug

Preliminary examination suggests that the jug was raised rather than cast. The surface was rather worn, as a result of cleaning or handling, giving a rather softened appearance to the detail. The base was folded inwards and is hollow on the underside.

The handle, which had apparently been soldered on (tests on the solder have not yet been completed), had been worked to shape, and the design inscribed with a gouge-shaped tool.

8 Inscribed bowl

The bowl had been raised, scraped on a lathe, and finally polished, probably on the lathe. The letters were engraved using a sharp tool which cut a crisp-edged round-bottomed groove. It was rather crudely done. There were signs of a previous rough out of the inscriptions.

9 Inscribed bowl

The original casting may have been of poor quality. The bowl was raised, possibly using the technique of crimp raising, and then scraped on a lathe. It was pre-polished radially and circumferentially, and finally polished. A punch was used for the inscription of the rim and base, probably a bar with a trumpet shape at either end. Where this could not be used (or half of it) the letters were chased. The inscription could be re-examined after cleaning.

10 Handled cup

The goblet had been raised, scraped and polished. The rim was thickened and may have been sawn or filed towards the inside to neaten it. The top and bottom are attached by means of a rod passing from one to the other via a hollow bead with flared ends. This may be of different composition from the rest of the goblet. It has not been possible to discover whether the rod is square sectioned throughout its length or only at the ends.

11 Gold disc with Chi-Rho

The disc was clipped from a piece of sheet; the design was worked on from both sides, having been drawn in (or inscribed) using a blunt-pointed tool and outlined on the other side.

10, 12, 13, 14, 16, 18, 19, 21, 22 Plaques with motifs

The leaves were made from thin sheet which was cut and further worked. The designs were inscribed from the back, (except No. 13 which was inscribed from the front), and the design outlined on the front. In some cases a compass had been used to inscribe the circle. The metal was not always of sound appearance (no. 16, 10) due to bands of impurities which resulted in spalling. Usually only the front surface was polished. The metal tended to be thinner at the most acute angled point. Holes near the point might be for suspending the leaves, but those at the centre of the circle seemed to be constructional. Leaves no. 10 and 18 were gilded.

Conclusion

The technology involved seems to be fairly simple, raising from an initial, suitably shaped casting, cleaning up and finishing on a lathe, with a final polish in some cases. Inscriptions have been applied by engraving, scribing (or chasing) and punching. Tools used for executing the designs included engraving tools, chaser (or scribers) punches and gouges. Soldering appeared to have been used but did not seem to have been especially favoured. Rivetting was used. Wire was not drawn.

APPENDIX B: The 1974 Water Newton Hoard

by Catherine M. Johns and R. A. G. Carson

This hoard was found on 24 February, 1974, in a field some 200 metres from the A1 road at Water Newton (Plate 31). A pottery bowl, covered by a lid, was found to contain a bronze bowl (used as a liner), two pieces of folded silver plate, remains of a linen-lined leather purse, and thirty Roman gold coins (Plate 31).[52]

Fig. 9 The Water Newton 1974 Treasure. Pottery bowl.

Fig. 10 The Water Newton 1974 Treasure. Pottery lid.

The pottery bowl (rim diameter 15·8 cm.) is burnished on the exterior and has a dark grey to black surface (Plate 33, Fig. 9). The upper part of the body is decorated by double lines in zig-zag pattern, enclosing in each triangle three impressed roundels. The style has been called 'Romano-Saxon'. The 'Castor box' lid (diameter 21·7 cm.) is a typical Nene Valley product (Plate 34, Fig. 10).

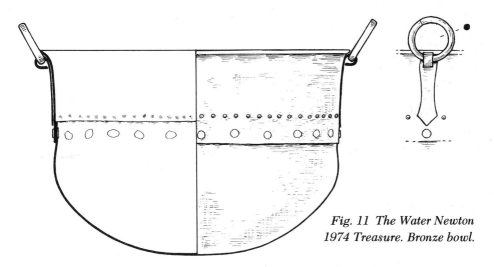

Fig. 11 The Water Newton 1974 Treasure. Bronze bowl.

The bronze bowl (diameter 13.5 cm., height 9 cm.) is of thin sheet bronze and consists of an upper band riveted to a lower part, formed from one piece of metal (Plate 35, Fig. 11). Two handles were found inside it, loose, their original points of attachment marked by patches of solder. The two pieces of folded silver plate weigh respectively 642 g. and 321 g. (Plate 32). The linen purse-lining is in plain weave.

The finding of a hoard of Roman gold coins in Britain is rare. Previously only four such hoards with secure documentation were on record, and none from the mid-fourth century, the date of this find. Although there are a few instances of silver coins hoarded with other silver objects, this is the first recorded find of gold coins hoarded with other precious metal objects. The thirty gold coins, all of the *solidus* denomination, the new gold unit introduced by Constantine I in AD 312, are of Constantine I and his sons, and represent issues between AD 330 and 350.

The coins fall into three chronological groups. The first group, four coins, was issued in the last years of the reign of Constantine I as Augustus and his three sons, Constantine II, Constantius and Constans as Caesars up to AD 337. The earliest coin, showing a little more wear than the others, is of Constantius II as Caesar, issued by the mint of Thessalonica in AD 330–31. Also in this group is the coin of Constantine I from the mint of Nicomedia in AD 335 and two *solidi* of Constans Caesar of about the same date from the Trier mint. The second group, only three coins, dates to AD 337–340 when the three sons of Constantine I divided the empire between them and reigned as joint Augusti. The single coin of the eldest, Constantine II, who controlled the western provinces, was struck at Trier. The one *solidus* of Constans, whose domain included Italy and the Balkans, was struck at Siscia. Although the third brother, Constantius II, had charge of the eastern provinces, his only coin in this group was issued at Aquileia in North Italy.

The bulk of the coins, 22 in number, falls in the third period between AD 340 when the death of Constantine II left his brother Constantius II and Constans to share the empire, and AD 350, when the revolt of Magnentius in the West removed Constans. The find contained no less than 14 *solidi* of Constans, five issued by the mint of Trier, three from Aquileia, five from Siscia and one from Thessalonica. Of the eight coins of Constantius II of this period only the one from Constantinople is from a mint in his own part of the empire. The balance is made up of a *solidus* from each of the mints of Thessalonica, Siscia and Aquileia, and four from Trier. The final piece, making up the total of thirty is a contemporary forgery of a *solidus* of Constans from the mint of Trier. The coin is up to the standard so far as weight is concerned, but is betrayed as a copy by the style of the obverse portrait and a small blunder in the inscription on the reverse.

The absence of any coins of Magnentius, who usurped power in the West in January AD 350, makes it fairly certain that the hoard was closed in that year, and presumably concealed then or shortly afterwards. There is no tradition of disturbance in the area at this date which might have occasioned the concealment of the hoard, and the explanation must lie in circumstances which we cannot readily discover.

The coin list[53]

AD 330-337

1 Constantine I, *RIC* vii, Nicomedia 179.
2 Constantius II, cf. *RIC* vii, Thessalonica 176.
3 Constans, *RIC* vii, Trier 575.
4 Constans, *RIC* vii, Trier 576.

AD 337–340

5 Constantine II, C.195, mint mark TR
6 Constantius II, C.63, mint mark SMAQ.
7 Constans, cf. C.147, *rev.* VICTORIA DN CONSTANTIS AVG, mint mark SIS*

AD 340–350

8 Constantius II, cf. C.67, *rev.* FELICITAS REIPVBLICE, mint mark CONS
9–12 Constantius II, cf. C.261, mint marks TR (3), TES (1)
13 Constantius II, C.280, mint mark TR
14 Constantius II, cf. C.283, but VOT XX MVL XXX, mint mark *S̄IS̄*
15 Constantius II, C.288, mint mark SMAQ
16–19 Constans, C.88, mint marks TR (2), SMAQ (2)
20 Constans, cf. C.89, but VOT X MVL XX, mint mark *S̄IS̄*
21–22 Constans, cf. C.60, but VOT X MVL XV, mint marks S̄IS̄*(1), . S̄IS̄* (1)
23–24 Constans, C.171 mint mark, T̄R̄
25–28 Constans, cf. C.174, but VOT X MVLT XX, mint marks T̄R̄ (1), S̄M̄ĀQ̄ (1) *S̄IS̄* (1), S̄IS̄. (1)
29 Constans, C.191, mint mark T̄ES̄
30 Constans, cf. C.153, mint mark T̄R̄ (contemporary copy)

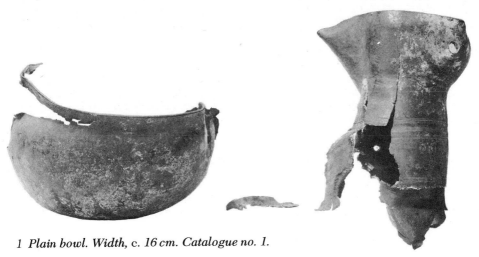

1 Plain bowl. Width, c. 16 cm. Catalogue no. 1.

2 Mouth and neck of spouted jug. Height, 10·5 cm. Catalogue no. 2.

3 Large dish. Diameter, 33·5 cm. Catalogue no. 3.

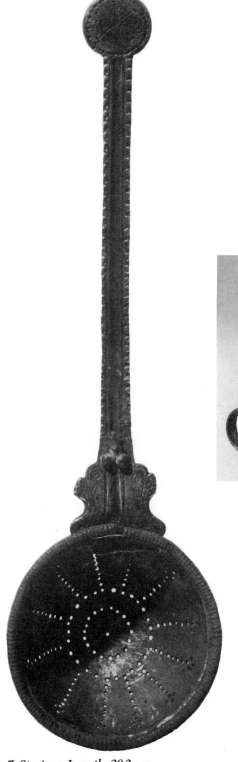

4 *Facetted bowl (from below).*
Diameter, c. 18–19 cm. Catalogue no. 4.

6 *Handled cup Height, 12·5 cm.*
Catalogue no. 6.

7 *Strainer. Length, 20·2 cm.*
Catalogue no. 7.

8 *Inscribed bowl. Diameter,*
c. 15 cm. Catalogue no. 8.

5 Decorated jug. Height, 20·3 cm. Catalogue no. 5.

9 Inscribed bowl. Diameter, 17 cm. Catalogue no. 9.

10 Plaque with Chi-Rho.
Height, 13·1 cm. Catalogue no. 10.

11 Gold disc with Chi-Rho.
Diameter, 4·9 cm. Catalogue no. 11.

12 *Plaque with Chi-Rho and inscription. Width, 10 cm. Catalogue no. 12.*

13 *Plaque with Chi-Rho (incuse).*
Height, 11·2 cm. Catalogue no. 13.

14 *Plaque with Chi-Rho.*
Height, 6·7 cm. Catalogue no. 14.

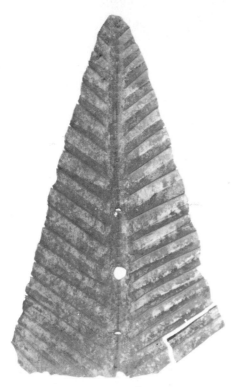

16 Plaque with Chi-Rho.
Height, 6·8 cm. Catalogue no. 16.

15 Plaque. Height, 7·4 cm.
Catalogue no. 15.

18 Plaque with Chi-Rho.
Height, 15·7 cm. Catalogue no. 18.

17 Plaque. Height, 7·8 cm.
Catalogue no. 17.

19 Plaque with Chi-Rho. Height, 4·9 cm. Catalogue no. 19.

22 Plaque with Chi-Rho. Height, 8 cm. Catalogue no. 22

*20 Plaque. Height, 5·8 cm.
Catalogue no. 20.*

*21 Plaque with Chi-Rho.
Height, 6 cm. Catalogue no. 21.*

23 Plaque. Height, 7 cm. Catalogue no. 23.

*24 Plaque. Height, 3·8 cm.
Catalogue no. 24.*

*26 Plaque. Height, 5·6 cm.
Catalogue no. 26.*

*25 Plaque. Height, 8 cm.
Catalogue no. 25.*

27 Plaque. Height, 5 cm. Catalogue no. 27.

28. Hypothetical reconstruction of the hoard as buried.

30 Aerial photograph of the town of Durobrivae *(Copyright reserved: Cambridge University Collection)*

29 Large dish with plaques as found.

31 *The Water Newton 1974 Treasure. (Reg. nos. P.1974, 6–1, 1 ff.)*

32 *The Water Newton 1974 Treasure. Folded silver plate. Height 10·5 cm.
(Reg. no. P.1974, 6–1, 4–5.)*

33 The Water Newton 1974 Treasure. Pottery bowl. Height 11·1 cm.
(Reg. no. P.1974, 6–1, 1.)

34 The Water Newton 1974 Treasure. Pottery lid. Height 9 cm.
(Reg. no. P.1974, 6–1, 2.)

*35 The Water Newton 1974 Treasure. Bronze bowl. Height 9 cm.
(Reg. no. P.1974, 6–1, 3.)*

Notes

1 The first formal presentation of the discovery was made at the Ninth International Congress of Christian Archaeology held at the Vatican in September, 1975, and a version of the paper is to be found in the *Rivista di Archeologia Christiana* LI (1975), p . 333–45, thanks to the kind encouragement and help of Father A. Ferrua.

2 These figures are the results of the first tests made for the purposes of the coroner's inquest. See Appendix A.

3 Dr J. P. Wild has pointed out that, to be precise, the treasure was found inside The Castles, the Roman town of *Durobrivae*, which is in Chesterton parish, while the 1974 hoard was found west of the town in Water Newton parish, the Billing Brook being the boundary. For a full discussion of the site see J. P. Wild, 'Roman Settlement in the Lower Nene Valley', *Archaeological Journal* CXXXI (1974), pp. 140–70; for a summary consideration of it in relation to other towns of Britain see J. Wacher, *The Towns of Roman Britain.* London, 1974, pp. 408–10.

4 D. E. Strong, *Greek and Roman, Gold and Silver Plate.* London, 1966, pp. 188–190.

5 O. M. Dalton, *Catalogue of the Early Christian Antiquities in the British Museum.* London, 1927, no. 344.

6 Alison Frantz, 'The Provenance of the Open Rho in the Christian Monograms', *American Journal of Archaeology,* 2nd series, (1929), pp. 10–26. Open rho: information in correspondence from Father Ferrua.

7 Strong, *op. cit.,* p. 175.

8 S. Loeschke, *Sammlung Niessen.* Köln, 1911, pl. 27, no. 328; C. W. Clairmont, *The Glass Vessels* (Ann Perkins, ed., *The Excavations at Dura-Europos,* Final Report IV Part V, New Haven 1963), pp. 60ff.

9 A. Kisa, *Das Glas im Altertume.* Leipzig, 1908, pp. 602–4 and fig. 208. The vessel is in the Hermitage Museum, Leningrad.

10 Strong, *op. cit.,* p. 170.

11 Professor T. J. Brown, Professor E. G. Turner and Dr W. E. H. Cockle pointed this out in a most helpful discussion. My colleague, T. Pattie, provided further invaluable assistance. Mistakes which can occur as a result of a craftsman working on stone from a patron's or a supervisor's draft are discussed by J. Marcillet-Jambert, 'Philologie et inscriptions', *Revue des Études Anciennes* LXII (1960), pp. 362–82.

12 Jean Mallon, *L'Écriture latine de la capitale romaine à la miniscule.* Paris, 1939.

13 The most notable examples of square capitals in the fourth century are those stone inscriptions cut in the third quarter of the century for Pope Damasus by Furius Dionysius Filocalus, who was also responsible for the *Calendar* of AD 354. Inscriptions for Pope Damasus: A. Ferrua, *Epigrammata Damasiana.* Città del Vaticano, 1942. Calendar: Henri Stern, *Le Calendrier de 354*, Institut français de Beyrouth, Bibliothèque archéologique et historique LV. Paris, 1953; K. Weitzmann, 'Book Illustration of the 4th Century, Tradition and Innovation', *Akten des VII Internationalen Kongresses für Christliche Archäologie, Trier 5–11 Sept., 1965* (Studi di antichità cristiana XII 1969), 264 ff.; Carl Nordenfalk, *Die spätantiken Zierbuchstaben.* Stockholm, 1970, pp. 83 ff.

14 J. M. C. Toynbee and J. B. Ward-Perkins, *The Shrine of St Peter and the Vatican Excavations.* London, 1956, pp. 175–8. For other Innocentii of the third and fourth centuries see A. H. M. Jones, J. R. Martindale and J. Morris, *The Prosopography of the Later Roman Empire, Vol. I, AD 260–395.* Cambridge, 1971, pp. 457–9.

15 A Cameron, *Claudian, Poetry and Propaganda at the Court of Honorius.* Oxford, 1970, pp. 287 ff.

16 Latin: F. J. E. Raby(ed.), *The Oxford Book of Mediaeval Latin Verse.* Oxford, 1958. Greek: C. A. Trypanis, *Medieval and Modern Greek Poetry.* Oxford, 1951.

17 J. A. Jungmann, *The Mass of the Roman Rite.* London, 1959, pp. 434–9.

18 Jungmann, *op. cit.,* pp. 210–11: 'In antiquity it was a natural practice to honour the temple by kissing the threshold. But it was also customary to greet the images of the gods by means of a kiss or to throw them a kiss from a distance, as the pagan Caecilius, mentioned by Minucius Felix, did when he noticed the statue of Serapis while passing by. In like manner the ancient altar was greeted with a kiss. And it seems that the family table, as a place enshrined by a religious dedication, was often similarly honoured at the start of a meal.'

19 Prostration: Jungmann, *op. cit.,* pp. 28, 52.

20 Gallic mass: Jungmann, *op. cit.,* pp. 34–5. From the sphere of Antioch-Syria we have the liturgy in the eighth book of the *Apostolic Constitutions,* also called the Clementine liturgy. It dates from the turn of the fourth century: Jungmann, p. 22. For the text see C. Kirch (ed.,) *Enchiridion Fontium Historiae Ecclesiasticae Antiquae,* 6th ed., L. Ueding. Barcelona, 1947, pp. 392–407.

21 F. J. Mone, *Lateinische und Griechische Messen aus dem zweiten bis sechsten Jahrhundert.* Frankfurt, 1850, pp. 1–72, especially (Missa VII), pp. 30–35.

22 Both plaques (*RIB* 986 and *RIB* 987) were dedicated to Cocidius: R. P. Wright and E. J. Phillips, *Catalogue of the Roman Inscribed and Sculptured Stones in Carlisle Museum, Tullie House,* 3rd edition. Carlisle, 1975, pp. 13–14, nos. 9 and 10.

23 R. Noll, 'An den Silbervotiven aus dem Dolichenusfund von Mauer a.d. Url', *Jahreshefte des Österreichischen archäologischen Instituts in Wien* (1950), cols. 125–46.

24 Kisa, *op. cit.,* p. 605. For the varying forms of the name Ancilla in African inscriptions see Marcillet-Jambert, Note 11, above.

25 M. J. T. Lewis, *Temples in Roman Britain.* Cambridge, 1966, pp. 99–107, with detailed references and bibliography.

26 Persecutions: H. Chadwick, *The Early Church.* Harmondsworth, 1967, pp. 116–25; W. H. C. Frend, *Martyrdom and Persecution in the Early Church.* Oxford, 1965.

27 W. H. C. Frend, 'The Christianization of Roman Britain', in M. W. Barley and R. P. C. Hanson (edd.), *Christianity in Britain, 300–700.* Leicester University Press, 1968, pp. 37–8.

28 Persecution of AD 303–4, action at Cirta, Numidia, 19 May, 303: *Gesta apud Zenophilum* in *Corpus Ecclesiasticorum Latinorum,* pp. 186–8. Objects confiscated in this police raid included the following books in the town, not at the church ('*scripturas plus non habemus quia subdiacones sumus; sed lectores habent codices'): codices quattuor [scripturas . . . domum Eugeni]; codices quinque [domum Felicis sarsoris]; codices octo [domum Victorini]; codices V maiores et minores II [domun Proiecti]; codices II et quiniones quattuor [Victor grammaticus]; codices VI [uxor Coddeonis].* Inside the church the officials found one book (*codicem unum);* but they confiscated many other objects: *calices duo aurei; calices sex argentei; urceola sex argentea* (amphorae); *cuccumellum argenteum* (pan); *lucernas argenteas septem; cereofala duo* (wax lights); *candelas breves aeneas cum lucernis suis septem; lucernas aeneas undecim cum catenis suis; tunicas muliebres LXXXII; mafortea XXXVIII* (veils); *tunicas viriles XVI; calligas viriles paria XIII; calligas muliebres paria XLVII; coplas rusticanas XVIIII* (thongs); *capitulatam argenteam* (small bust); *lucermam argenteam; dolia IIII; arcaeVI.*

29 Constantius Chlorus: J. Vogt, 'Pagans and Christians in the Family of Constantine the Great', in A. Momigliano (ed.), *The Conflict between Paganism and Christianity in the Fourth Century.* Oxford, 1963, pp. 43–4.

30 Strong, *op. cit.*, pp. 128–9; *Mitteilungen des deutschen archäologischen Instituts, Römische Abteilung,* 36–37, 1921–22, pp. 34 ff.

31 Optatus, *On the Schism of the Donatists* I, 15–19.

32 J. M. C. Toynbee, *Art in Britain under the Romans.* Oxford, 1964, pp. 301–3.

33 E. Babelon, *Le Trésor de Berthouville.* Paris, 1920, pp. 14–32.

34 H. B. Walters, *Catalogue of the Silver Plate, Greek, Etruscan and Roman, in the British Museum.* London, 1921, nos. 144–82.

35 Kaiseraugst: R. Laur-Belart, *Der spätrömische Silberschatz von Kaiseraugst.* Basel, 1963. Mildenhall: J. W. Brailsford, *The Mildenhall Treasure.* London, 1947; K. S. Painter, 'The Mildenhall Treasure: A Reconsideration', *British Museum Quarterly* XXXVII (1973), pp. 154–80. Esquiline: O. M. Dalton, *Catalogue of the Early Christian Antiquities in the British Museum.* London 1927.

36 C. M. Johns and R. Carson, 'The Water Newton Hoard', in *Durobrivae: A Review of Nene Valley Archaeology* 3 (1975), pp. 10–12, and appendix.

37 S. S. Frere, *Britannia, A History of Roman Britain.* London, 1967, pp. 349 ff.

38 The Water Newton silver is not matched in the hoard of AD 317 from Jugoslavia, nor that of AD 321–2 from the Eastern Roman Empire, now in Munich. Both these hoards, however, are essentially *largitio* plates, distributed on the occasion of imperial anniversaries, and their basic difference in character would preclude them from direct comparison with the Water Newton hoard, were it not that a bowl of the same form but with a Christian inscription has been found at Montbellet, France, with a Christian inscription, ZESES IN XPO DOMINO VINCENTI. Jugoslavia: Strong, *op. cit.* pp. 199–201. Munich: B. Overbeck, *Argentum Romanum, Ein Schatzfund von spätrömischen Prunkgeschirr.* Munich, 1973; Montbellet (Saône-et-Loire): information from Monsieur L. Bonnamour, and F. Baratte in *Journal des Savants* (1975), pp. 193–212; esp. p. 206.

39 Athanasius, *Apologia Contra Arianos* (Migne, XXV), paras. 60 ff., and especially para. 11: *Cum igitur neque ibi Ecclesia esset, neque qui sacra faceret, neque dies hoc ipsum requireret, quale, aut quando, aut ubinam mysticum poculum fractum est? Nam pocula esse per domos, et in medio foro, patet; quae si quis frangat nullatenus inpie agit. Mysticum vero poculum, quod si quis sponte fregerit, pro tali ausu impius efficitur, apud solos legitimos Ecclesiae praesides invenitur: hic enim solus huius poculi usus et non alius est.* See also : A. H. M. Jones, *Constantine and the Conversion of Europe.* Harmondsworth, 1962, pp. 178–9.

40 Toynbee, *op. cit.*, pp. 328–31; Noll, *op. cit.*; Walters, *op. cit.*, nos. 224–41; O. Doppelfeld (ed.), *Römer am Rhein.* Cologne, 1967, pp. 246–8.

41 The churches as juristic persons capable of proprietary rights: (a) Eusebius, *Historia Ecclesiastica* 7, 13, 2: rescript of Gallienus on restoration of Christians' property, AD 260; *Codex Theodosianus* 16.2.4: edict of Constantine on legacies to the Church, AD 321; *Codex Theodosianus* 14, 3, 11: mandate of Valentinian I and Valens on exclusion of bakers from the clericate, AD 365; P. R. Coleman-Norton, *Roman State and Christian Church.* London, 1966, nos. 4, 36, 133. *Refrigeria:* J. M. C. Toynbee and J. B. Ward-Perkins, *The Shrine of St Peter and the Vatican Excavations.* London, 1956, p. 178.

42 Cyprian, *Op. eleem.* XV: *Locuples et dives es et dominicum celebrare te credis, quae corban omino non respicis, quae in dominicum sine sacrificio venis, quae partem de sacrificio quod pauper optulit' (PL* IV 612, 613, *CSEL* III 384). The reference by Cyprian relates most probably only to wine and bread: V. Saxer, *Vie Liturgique et Cotidienne à Carthage vers le Milieu du IIIᵉ Siècle* (Studi di Antichità Cristiana XXIX). Vatican, 1969, pp. 245-8.

43 J. A. Jungmann, *The Mass of the Roman Rite.* London, 1959, pp. 319–20.

44 *Altare* in the sense of 'shrine', 'sanctuary', 'sacred place': J. M. C. Toynbee and J. B. Ward-Perkins, *op. cit.*, pp. 212 ff.; A. Ferrua, *Epigrammata Damasiana.* Vatican, 1942, p. 122, 1.5; Gregory of Tours, *De Gloria Martyrum* XXVIII (Migne, *Patrologia Latina* LXXI, cols. 728–9), and *Historia Francorum* II, 14 (Migne, *Patrologia Latina* LXXI, col. 213). Oblations: Irenaeus, *Adversus Haereses,* ed. W. W. Harvey. Cambridge, 1857, IV, 21, 5; Jungmann, *op. cit.*, pp. 317 ff.; A. H. Couratin, 'Liturgy', in R. P. C. Hanson (ed.), *Historical Theology.* Harmondsworth. 1969, pp. 153–4.

45 M. J. T. Lewis, *Temples in Roman Britain.* Cambridge, 1966. p. 35. Britain: Verulamium 1; Frilford 2; Brean Down, Bruton; Springhead 1. France: Cracouville (Eure); Poitiers. Germany: temple of Mars Lenus at Trier. For parallels in early Christian churches see T. F. Mathews, *The Early Churches of Constantinople: Architecture and Liturgy.* Pennsylvania State University Press, 1971, pp. 156 ff.

46 Jungmann, *op. cit.*, pp. 122 ff.

47 See particularly the Gallican mass, described by Jungmann, *op. cit.*, pp. 225 ff. Missa IV of the Gallican form is even written in hexameters.

48 A. H. M. Jones, *The Later Roman Empire 284–602.* Oxford, 1964, pp. 172, 781–8.

49 *Vita S. Melaniae Junioris* (Greek), in *Analecta Bollandia* XXII (1903), 7–49, especially 11–12, 19–21, 37. Melania's large estates: *Vita S. Melaniae Junioris* (Latin), in *Analecta Bollandia* VII (1889), 19–63. She and her husband were also notable supporters of Pelagius: P. Brown, *Augustine of Hippo.* London, 1967, pp. 340–41; *idem., Religion and Society in the Age of Saint Augustine.* London, 1972, pp. 212 ff.

50 D. B. Harden, 'Late Roman Wheel-Inscribed Glasses with Double-Line letters', *Kölner Jahrbuch* IX (1967–1968), pp. 43–55; K. S. Painter, 'A. Roman Christian Silver Treasure from Biddulph, Staffordshire', *Antiquaries Journal* LV (1975), pp. 62–9, especially pp. 67–8.

51 Canoscio: E. Giovagnoli, 'Una Collezione di Vasi Eucaristici Scoperti a Canoscio', *Rivista di Archeologia Cristiana* XII (1935), pp. 313–28; E. Giovagnoli, *Il Tesoro Eucaristico di Canoscio.* Città di Castello, 1940. Kumluca: N. Firatli, 'Un Trésor du sixieme siècle trouvé à Kumluca, en Lycie', *Akten des VII Internationalen Kongresses fur Christliche Archäologie, Trier, 1965.* Trier, 1969, pp. 523–5; Ekrem Akurgal, Cyril Mango, Richard Ettinghausen, *Die Türkei und ihre Kunstschätze.* Geneva, 1966, pp. 98–101; *Handbook of the Byzantine Collection, Dumbarton Oaks.* Washington, 1967, nos. 63–70, pp. 18–20.

52 The first account of this hoard (Registration no. P.1974, 6-1, 1 ff.) was published in *Durobrivae: A Review of Nene Valley Archaeology* 3 (1975), pp. 10–12. See also R. A. G. Carson, 'The Water Newton hoard of gold solidi', in *The British Museum Yearbook* 1: *The Classical Tradition* (1976), pp. 219–20. The hoard is now in the collections of the British Museum. The coins and silver plate were declared Treasure Trove. The other objects were presented by Mr R. H. Waterworth.

53 References in the list are abbreviated thus: (a) *RIC* vii: *Roman Imperial Coinage* VII. London, 1966; C: H. Cohen, *Descripton historique des monnaies frappées sous l'empire romain,* Paris, 1880.